pocket
cornwall

CW00701432

St Ives and St Ives Bay

David Chapman

Alison Hodge

First published in 2009 by
Alison Hodge, 2 Clarence Place, Penzance,
Cornwall TR18 2QA, UK
info@alison-hodge.co.uk
www.alison-hodge.co.uk

ISBN-13 978-0-906720-65-3

British Library Cataloguing-in-Publication Data
A catalogue record for this book is available from
the British Library.

Designed and originated by
BDP – Book Development & Production,
Penzance, Cornwall

Printed in China

Title page: Godrevy from Porthminster Beach

Contents

Introduction

Boats in the harbour (facing page)
Sunbathing and playing on St Ives beaches (above)

Small streets, appealing alleyways and stacked steps create a maze of interest. A harbour, packed with boats, bristles with enthralling activity. Beaches of clean white sand face in every direction, attracting people to sit, eat, read, paint and play; the sea, crystal clear and inviting, acts as a focus for a huge range of pursuits from surfing to paddling and swim-

Small cobbled street in the town (above). Godrevy from St Ives (facing page). St Ives in sea mist (overleaf)

ming to boating. The seasons and weather, ever-changing, cloud and sunlight playing with colour, shadow and form. Location, near the tip of the most south-westerly point in Britain, and yet on the shore of a spectacular and sheltered bay, with its sweeping dune systems, estuary and the distant, distinctive landmark of Godrevy Lighthouse. And finally its people, enthusiastic and involved, making this a true community, and yet welcoming hundreds of thousands of visitors to share their town every year. This is St Ives.

The crystal-clear sea, white sand and blue sky in St Ives (far left) are in stark contrast to a winter storm (left). People gather around the Sloop Inn for a late evening drink (above)

In this book I aim to offer a taste of life in St Ives through the course of a year. Using my camera, I would like to introduce you to its annual festivities; a little of its history; its popular attractions; its changing moods; its bay; its wildlife; its people, and even its nightlife.

David Chapman, 2009

Around Town

There is no better place to start a visit to St Ives than around the harbour. The main pier, known as Smeaton's Pier, was constructed during the eighteenth and nineteenth centuries. It was originally much shorter than it is today; the lighthouse which is now half way along the pier was once at its very end.

The first phase of construction, in the latter part of the eighteenth century, created a pier 110 m long, which was made of 35,000

tonnes of stone. It was designed by John Smeaton and built by Thomas Richardson, the pair who had previously created the Eddystone Lighthouse. John Smeaton was reputedly the first civil engineer with a string of construction successes to his name: bridges, canals and, most notably, the Forth & Clyde Canal.

In 1860, the original pier was increased in length with a wooden extension, but this failed within 20 years, so in the 1890s the pier was again extended, but this time with stone, taking the entire length to 200 m. The three arches in the pier were added at this point to allow the sea to wash sand through the harbour, so preventing it from silting up.

At the foot of the pier is St Leonard's mediaeval chapel, where fishermen would have said their prayers before venturing to sea. Inside this small sanctuary is a modest collection of model fishing boats.

By the mid-fourteenth century, even before the building of the current significant harbour walls, St Ives was the biggest fishing port in Penwith. As early as the fifteenth century it had its own weekly market to sell the fish. St Ives harbour, like many other Cornish harbour towns, had a strong association with

Smeaton's Pier (facing page).
The lighthouse (left)

Smeaton's Pier, looking towards Porthgwidden

the pilchard fishery. From about the fifteenth century through to the 1920s, pilchards were caught from, and processed in, the town. In its heyday there were 400 pilchard fishing boats stationed here, but the pilchards were over-fished and simply do not occur in the same numbers any more. On one day in December 1920, a good catch brought in a staggering 2,000,000 pilchards! The pilchards were processed in pressing yards often right on the water's edge. They were laid out with salt to cure them, and would be left there for a few months.

To enable the fishermen at sea to find the largest shoals of fish, they would have used the behaviour of birds such as gannets as an indicator. They also had the assistance of a huer on the cliffs. A huer would find a high vantage point from which to look for signs of

Fishing boats still use St Ives harbour (above and overleaf). A gannet (right)

the disturbance caused by huge shoals, and would then direct the fishermen towards the fish using hand signals. As this system developed, huers' huts were built around the county in high places overlooking the sea. Many were made of wood, but in St Ives the huer's lookout, overlooking Porthminster Point, is of stone, and is painted white.

The James Stevens no. 10 *returns to harbour from a pleasure cruise*

Today the harbour is still busy with small boats, particularly in summer when there are plenty of mackerel in the sea. There is also the potential to take pleasure trips on board old boats such as the *James Stevens no. 10*, which was built in 1899 and served St Ives as a lifeboat for 33 years, saving 227 lives; or the *Dolly Pentreath*, a traditional Cornish lugger built in St Ives in 1993 from plans for an old lugger, *The Godrevy*. The *Dolly Pentreath* was named after the (reputedly) last speaker of the Cornish language, who was born in Mousehole and died in 1777. Trips go to Seal Island, among others, though seals often frequent the harbour at high tide.

The seals seen in St Ives are all grey seals, and they have become quite accustomed to the presence of fishermen and other people, readily taking fish from onlookers. In summer, large groups of people can gather to watch the seals from Smeaton's Pier. In fact, the harbour area is very popular with a wide range of wildlife, which often becomes very tame because of the sheer number of people milling around. Turnstones are the small wading birds that have taken to running up and down the harbour walls as well as along the roads and footpaths around the harbour. They can be found in most months of the year, except possibly May and June.

A grey seal seen from the harbour wall (above)
A turnstone runs along the pavement (right)

The gulls that have learnt to steal chips, pasties and ice-creams, are herring gulls. They have become quite a menace, but it is only through our teaching that they have adopted these disturbing tactics, and it will take us a long time to train them to stop. Other species of gull in the harbour regularly include lesser black-backed and great black-backed gulls, which are rarely seen in many other parts of the country.

On the streets around the Sloop Inn, look out for starlings. These delightful birds have an iridescent sheen to their plumage, and a wonderful range of songs, occasionally mimicking sounds from their environment.

Moving on from the harbour, another significant landmark in St Ives has become known as The Island. Like many other distinctive Cornish headlands, this was a promontory fort in the Iron Age, and would have had a ditch and rampart defence, though its shape makes it an ideal defensive position even without any artificial additions. Before it was known as 'The Island', this headland was known by the name Pendinas, which means 'a fortified headland'.

The Island was again fortified from about 1638, having up to 15 guns present. The granite battery walls were built in 1860, and housed three canons to defend against French invasion during the Napoleonic wars. The nearby cottage was originally the barracks. The coastguard lookout, located within the battery, was operated by HM Coastguard until 1994. After operations ceased, the National Coastwatch Institution (NCI), a voluntary organization, began operating here in 1999. Where the NCI station now stands there was once a tall pole fitted with a lantern, which served as a guide to local

A pair of herring gulls, and a great black-backed gull on the beach in winter (facing page)
A starling shows off its iridescent plumage (above)
Porthmeor Beach and The Island (overleaf)

fishermen returning at night. This is why the promontory at the north-east end of The Island is called Lamp Rock. Also on The Island is the chapel of St Nicholas, which dates back to the fifteenth century, though the present chapel was rebuilt in 1911.

Facing page, clockwise from top left: The chapel of St Nicholas, the Coastguard lookout, and a view from The Island towards Clodgy Point. Bottlenose dolphins are often seen from The Island (above)

From The Island the views are remarkable. It is possible to see as far as Trevose Head, some 26 miles east along the north coast, and there is a fantastic view of St Ives Bay and towards Clodgy Point to the west. This is a great place to sit and watch the sea, and as well as watching waves and clouds passing by it is also possible, occasionally, to spot dolphins and sea birds. Sea birds (such as shearwaters, terns, auks and skuas) can get blown into St Ives Bay and are forced to fly close to The Island on their exit towards the open sea. This is one of the best places in the whole of the county for seeing dolphins: I have seen bottlenose dolphins leaping and playing in the vigorous currents adjacent to The Island on many occasions. Also seen occasionally is the more docile harbour porpoise, though calmer days are more productive for sightings of these less playful creatures.

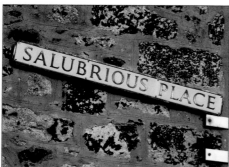

Looking down Fore Street (above), and Salubrious Place (left)

Much of the appeal of St Ives lies tucked away in its cobbled back streets. Inland from the harbour is Fore Street, at the heart of the town, where the Primitive Methodist Church can be found. Methodism has a strong tradition in St Ives – the fishing and mining communities were always a stronghold of this religion. The most famous of all Methodist

*The Primitive Methodist Church (left and below),
and a glimpse into Fore Street from Virgin Street*

preachers, John Wesley, first visited the town
in 1743, and returned to preach here on 27
occasions.

Wander along the myriad small alleyways
from Fore Street, and wonder at the strange
and sometimes perplexing names they bear.
The Digey may well refer to the practice
of dying fishing nets to preserve them, but

One of the many fascinating shops in Fore Street (left). A view up Virgin Street from Fore Street (right)

others, such as Salubrious Place, Court Cocking and Virgin Street are only to marvel at!

Many of the streets between Fore Street and Tate St Ives host art galleries and craft

A gallery on The Digey (left). The Salthouse Gallery, Norway Square (right)

shops, but the architecture of the old houses and streets are as much a work of art as the paintings and sculptures which take pride of place in the galleries. Look out in particular

Glimpses of the old town. The ancient granite arch at Hicks Court, off The Digey (facing page, top right) is a St Ives icon, as are its many cats (bottom right)

for the granite arch to Hicks Court. This is the entrance to the place where George Hicks once lived: he was portreeve (or port warden) of St Ives from 1611 to 1624, and the arch is always popular with photographers.

Colourful buoys and boat fenders adorn Norway House in Norway Square – a reminder that you are never far from the sea in St Ives!

Contrasting with the greys of the old granite buildings and slate roofs of the town, are brightly painted doors and shutters; colourful, decorated corners, and jewel-like courtyards. St Ives has won the 'Britain in Bloom' competition, organized by the Royal Horticultural Society (RHS), many times. Look around the streets of the town in summer, and you will see hanging baskets full of bright flowers; terracotta pots lining alleys and steps, and flow-

Turn a corner in St Ives during the summer, and you are likely to come across jewel-like gardens (above left and overleaf), with Mediterranean and subtropical plants

erbeds in the public areas carefully tended and crammed with colour, texture and pattern. Subtropical plants thrive in the temperate climate in a town which rarely experiences frost. The floral displays, together with the lovingly tended cottages and gardens, help to make this a town that people readily take to their hearts. There cannot be many towns where the 'back streets' are so inspirational and such a delight!

The harbour beach in St Ives (left), and Tate St Ives, above Porthmeor Beach (right)

Apart from the beach in the harbour, there are three other beaches in St Ives, offering you the chance to find a sheltered spot in just about any weather conditions. On the north coast of the town is the most exposed of the beaches, known as Porthmeor Beach ('Great Cove' beach). This long beach faces directly out into the Atlantic, and is therefore usually the best spot in town for surfing.

Inland of the beach is the now famous gallery, Tate St Ives. This smooth, white three-storey building was completed in 1993, transforming the site of an old gas storage tank and bringing a touch of the Mediterra-

Inside the entrance of Tate St Ives

nean to the shore of Porthmeor Beach. The columns and rotunda set the scene for the space and light that this building brings to its gallery areas. Stand in the circular entrance to the gallery on a stormy day and you will feel that the waves are breaking around your ears. The design of this feature helps to make the building a part of its wider environment. Inside the gallery are permanent collections of modernist work by artists associated with St Ives and the surrounding area from the 1920s onwards, as well as work by contemporary artists.

On the hill behind Tate St Ives is Barnoon Cemetery. It is worth climbing the steep steps beside the gallery, and crossing the car park to admire not only the view but also the memorial stones in the cemetery. There are many fine headstones of carved Cornish

Barnoon Cemetery, looking out over Porthmeor Beach, with Carrick Du to the left

granite, and of particular interest is the grave of Alfred Wallis, 'artist and mariner'. In the 1920s, the naive paintings of this retired fisherman and scrap dealer inspired the London artists who visited St Ives. Wallis died a pauper, but his grave is covered in decorated, glazed tiles made by the potter Bernard Leach, one of the many artists who settled in St Ives at this time.

A short walk to the west of Porthmeor Beach brings us to the small rocky headland of Carrick Du, and a little further on is Clodgy Point. It was just offshore here, in 1939, that the St Ives lifeboat foundered in extremely

Barnoon Cemetery: granite headstones (left), and Alfred Wallis's grave (right). There can be few cemeteries so magnificently sited

The rocks of Carrick Du lashed by a storm

heavy seas. She overturned three times, eventually throwing all of her crew overboard. Only one survived: William Freeman astonishingly made it to shore at Godrevy.

Sandwiched between The Island and the harbour is the small beach of Porthgwidden ('White Cove'), sheltered on either side by rocks, and behind by white beach huts.

Probably the most popular beach with summer visitors is Porthminster – a Cornish name meaning a 'cove with a church'. Here groups of volunteers spend summer days helping children to enjoy their holidays, playing games such as tug-of-war. Overlooked by some of the town's largest hotels and adjacent to the railway station, this beach is often very busy on hot summer days.

Porthgwidden, with its white beach huts, and The Island (left). A view over Porthminster Beach in winter (right), and Porthminster Beach in summer (below)

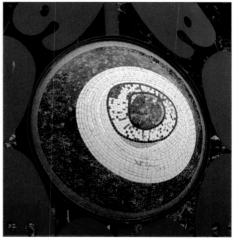

Clockwise from left: Boarding a train at St Ives railway station; colourful summer blooms, and a sculpture by local artist David Kemp

The bench ends in the parish church

Just above Porthminster Beach is St Ives station. The railway line connecting St Ives to the main line at St Erth was built from 1874, with four stations along its route. St Ives station was removed in 1971, leaving simply a station platform which is used by a huge number of people in the summer months. This service operates as a park-and-ride from Lelant, helping to reduce congestion in St Ives and offering a unique and beautiful way of approaching the town.

One of the main focal points of St Ives is provided by the parish church, consecrated in 1434 and dedicated to St Ia, an Irish priestess after whom the town is named. The tower of the church is over 24 m tall, and is made of Cornish granite. Inside, look carefully at the heavy, dark bench ends which, with their deep carvings, are typical of mediaeval Cornish work. Within the church there is a second isle, known as the Lady Chapel or Trenwith Aisle. It was built between 1450 and 1500 and restored in the twentieth century.

Hepworth's Madonna and Child *in the parish church (left), and* Epidaurous, *on the Malakoff (right)*

The 'Lady' of the chapel is the Blessed Virgin Mary, and appropriately within the church stands a sculpture, *Madonna and Child*, which was carved by Dame Barbara Hepworth in memory of her son, Paul Skeaping, who died in active service with the RAF over Thailand in 1953.

Barbara Hepworth's work is intrinsically linked to West Cornwall, which inspired much of her sculpture. Her abstract forms explored the natural landscape around her, and we need look no further than the granite headlands around the county's coast to see that inspiration for ourselves. She lived in

Some of the many craft shops and galleries in St Ives

St Ives from 1939 until her death in 1975. From 1949, she lived and worked at the Trewyn Studio, which is now the Barbara Hepworth Museum and Sculpture Garden, and part of Tate St Ives. We can visit Hepworth's studio and garden and see many of her absorbing pieces in an intimate setting. There are also Hepworth sculptures outside the Guildhall and on the Malakoff, overlooking the town, as well as the one in the parish church.

The name of St Ives is now synonymous with art; the town with its wonderful quality of light has attracted artists for many years, the first school of painting being established here in the late nineteenth century. Perhaps the peak was in the mid-twentieth century, when Barbara Hepworth, Ben Nicholson and many others, including the potter Bernard Leach, worked in the town. Their legacy remains in the countless art galleries; the most famous is undoubtedly Tate St Ives,

Victorian town houses

but the many others scattered around in the small streets of the town help to provide a unique character. The Leach Pottery, at Higher Stennack on the outskirts of the town, was set up by Bernard Leach – a pioneer artist potter in Britain – and the Japanese potter Shoji Hamada in 1920. In recent years, the Leach Restoration Project restored and developed the pottery, and it now has new workshops and exhibition space.

Standing on the harbour, or even on the Malakoff, looking into the town of St Ives, it is impossible not to be struck by the rows of terraced town houses. These were built during the late nineteenth and early twentieth centuries, and stand on ground which was once the domain of Cornish tinners. Among these newer buildings remain some older, eighteenth-century buildings which would have been home to the miners. Tin stream-

The view from the Malakoff (above). Rosewall Hill (below). St Ives from Rosewall Hill (overleaf)

ing was once prevalent on the banks of the River Stennack, and the valley would have been an industrial landscape, completely different from that which we see today.

Looking up the Stennack valley from St Ives, we see the significant landmark of Rosewall Hill. On top of this hill are some wonderful granite sculptures created by the effects of wind and rain finding weaknesses which even this hard rock possesses. On the hill we can see the remains of Rosewall Mine, and a walk to the summit reveals a whole manner of workings with shafts and bare rocky ground all around the summit, as well as tremendous views over St Ives Bay.

St Ives Bay

Godrevy Lighthouse in a storm

St Ives is situated on the shore of St Ives Bay, the whole of which can be seen from the town. The great sweeping arc of the bay provides a sheltered haven for wildlife, and much historical interest around its edge.

Directly across the bay from St Ives is situated the iconic landmark of Godrevy Lighthouse. It was the loss of the *Nile*, a 700-ton steamer with all her crew and passengers, in 1854 that led to the construction of the lighthouse. Building began in early 1858,

Gwithian Beach

and the 26-m tower was first illuminated in March 1859. It was modernized in 1995, and is now powered by solar energy. The lighthouse was built on an island just off shore. The sea around here can be treacherous, with strong currents, just as it can be around The Island in St Ives, but this makes it attractive to wildlife. Grey seals, for exam-ple, are also found in this area, and you can look down into Mutton Cove, near Godrevy Head, to see groups of up to 100 grey seals hauled out to bask in the sun.

From Godrevy to the south there is a superb, long beach of sand backed by dunes, or towans as they are known in Cornwall. These towans are at their lowest near to Godrevy, where they have been influenced

St Ives Bay from Upton Towans, with remains of the dynamite factory in the left foreground

by the outflow of the Red River and by sand extraction. The sand extraction ceased recently, and the area has been turned into a nature reserve called St Gothian Sands. South of here is a long stretch of flat sand between Gwithian and Hayle, an area popular with surfers, sand-yachters and kite-surfers. Adjacent to Gwithian is the nature reserve of Upton Towans, which belongs to the Cornwall Wildlife Trust (CWT). Here it is still possible to see the remains of a dynamite factory, which was operational from 1890 to 1917. Look for rectangular banks, made to protect the processing buildings from accidental blasts in neighbouring processes.

The towans are rich in wildlife. Of particular note are the flowers which occur here, including pyramidal orchid, autumn lady's tresses, bird's-foot trefoil, wild thyme, biting stonecrop, common stork's bill, viper's bugloss, sea holly and sea spurge. Butterflies include the silver-studded blue and dark green fritillary. Also watch out for reptiles, including adders which can be numerous here.

The towans are broken by Hayle Estuary. This was once a busy port for fishing, as well

as importing and exporting various materials associated with the power station and foundries that were operational here. It is now a quiet harbour, and most of the estuary is owned by the Royal Society for the Protection of Birds (RSPB). This is a significant staging post for wading birds, with many thousands of them spending the winter here.

Progressing over the estuary, another sandy beach, known as Porth Kidney, is backed by the towans of Lelant. Lelant was an important port in mediaeval times, and around the edge of the Hayle Estuary it is still possible to see evidence of the quays that were used, as well as the remains of many old boats.

On the towans there is a golf course, owned by West Cornwall Golf Club and, adjacent to this, the parish church of Lelant, St Uny. The church is partly Norman, but was restored and updated in the thirteenth and fifteenth centuries. The churchyard has many Cornish crosses, and is an example of a 'Living Churchyard' in which wildflowers are encouraged to grow. St Uny was an Irish saint, who was probably here in the sixth century AD. Lelant also has connections with St Anta, from whom its name derives: the first written version of its name was Lananta.

Lelant Towans are rich in wildlife, though it appears they were also once a significant

Clockwise from top left: pyramidal orchid, viper's bugloss, autumn lady's tresses, a pair of silver-studded blue butterflies, dark green fritillary, and sea spurge – all found on the towans

The Hayle Estuary, with the St Ives train running alongside (above)
Porth Kidney Sands and Lelant Towans (overleaf)

ritual site for our ancestors, as many human remains were found when the railway line was constructed in 1875. Many of these now lie under the golf course which was created in 1890.

Between Lelant Towans and Hawke's Point, the coast path is cloaked in densely packed trees, this being in marked contrast to the rest of the bay. The path rises high on the cliff tops before descending down again

St Uny Church at Lelant and the golf course, seen from Hayle harbour in winter

to the beach at Carbis Bay, once known as Barrepta Cove.

The safe, sheltered beach of Carbis Bay is a gentle, sandy link between the two substantial headlands of Hawke's Point and Porth-minster Point, and is popular with tourists in the summer. Its popularity grew in Victorian times with the advent of the rail link, and initially a few houses for visitors were con-structed in the wooded Carbis Valley. Tour-

The beach at Carbis Bay

ists were encouraged to walk from St Ives to visit Hawke's Point and the nearby holy well and grotto. Carbis Bay was once part of the parish of Lelant, but was separated in the early twentieth century as it grew in size.

St Ives Festivals

Each year in St Ives there is a regular pro-
gramme of festivals and events. Some have a
religious significance; others are planned with
a view to entertaining tourists; some raise
money for charities, and a few simply allow
the locals to let off steam!

St Ives Feast Day (February)

Feast Day always falls on the first Monday
after 3 February. This marks the anniversary
of the consecration of the Parish Church of
St Ia in 1434. St Ia was an Irish woman who
came to Cornwall in a coracle from Ireland in
the fifth century AD. She set about convert-
ing all the pagans of St Ives, and the town was
subsequently named after her.

Events to celebrate this religious conver-
sion of the town include a procession led by
the Mayor of St Ives. The Mayor takes a silver
ball from the Guildhall through the streets of
the town, followed by a variety of people,
including a small band and lots of dancing chil-

*The mayor and other dignitaries prepare to walk
to the holy well*

Children dance on the route, and music is played along the way

dren. The procession wends its way to St Ia's Well near Porthmeor Beach, where a short service is held. It then returns to the parish church and the Mayor throws the silver ball

The mayor throws the silver ball. A crowd gathers to try to catch it, and youngsters run away across the beach with it

The hunt gathers (left). The silver ball (right)

into a waiting crowd of children on the beach below. The children fight over the ball, and it changes hands several times before being returned to the Mayor at midday in return for a small reward. Meanwhile, the Western Hunt meets in Royal Square and many children gather at the Guildhall to be presented with pennies by the Mayor. One or two other events happen around town during the day, but those are the ones with the greatest historical significance.

Good Friday

Hellesveor Chapel, and yachting on Consols Pool

A wonderful family day takes place on Good Friday at Hellesveor Chapel, on the outskirts of St Ives at the top of the Stennack. The day begins with model boat sailing on Consols Pool adjacent to the chapel. This dates back to a time when seafarers would sail miniature boats on the sea during the spring as an offering of peace to the 'God of the Storms', in the hope that they would be able to sail safely through the summer. The tradition at Consols Pool is still upheld by quite a large gathering of people, many of whom stay at the chapel for refreshments in the morning, a service in the afternoon and then a 'faith tea' in the late afternoon. A faith tea involves each member of the community bringing something to the table for everyone to share.

Mayday Celebrations

The May Queen is crowned (above). A colourful crowd of supporters (overleaf)

More pomp and ceremony sees a May Queen chosen and crowned outside the Guildhall, where speeches from the Mayor and other dignitaries are addressed to the crowd. Afterwards a procession of various groups of people, children from local schools, dancers and musicians, led by the Mayor, passes through the town.

Midsummer Bonfire

The midsummer bonfire is organized by the Old Cornwall Society, which, incidentally, was formed in St Ives, in 1920. It takes place on the evening (approximately 9.30 pm) of 23 June each year, currently at Higher Carn Stabba Farm. It involves an ancient ceremony to pray for a good harvest. Part of the occasion involves throwing bad weeds as well as productive plants on to the fire, and offering prayers to promote the growth of the good plants while reducing the growth of the weeds.

The Biathlon

The Biathlon is organized annually by the St Ives Surf Life Saving Club, in early July. It serves as a fundraising event, and consists of a 2 km run along the coast from the Sloop Inn towards Carbis Bay, followed by a swim back across the bay of approximately the same distance. The record for the event, to date, is 32 minutes and 35 seconds.

Participants running in the biathlon

The John Knill Celebrations

John Knill was born in Callington in 1733. He became the collector of customs in St Ives from 1762 to 1782, and was town mayor in 1767. In 1782, he built his own mausoleum. Situated on Worvas Hill, it is known as the Knill's Monument, or Knill's Steeple. It was his intention to be buried in his mausoleum, but Knill died in London and was actually buried at Holborn.

In his will he left money for the upkeep of the mausoleum, and for celebrations to be held every five years. The parade of people includes: ten little girls; the Mayor, vicar and head of customs; a fiddler and two widows. These people and various other guests walk from the Guildhall to the monument. The money that Knill set aside also included £5 to be given to the couple that has raised the greatest family of legitimate children, each to have reached the age of ten years!

Finishing the swim with a sprint up to the Sloop

Knill's Monument by night (facing page)

Lifeboat Day

Usually held in August to coincide with the maximum number of tourists in the town, Lifeboat Day is a fundraising event for the Royal National Lifeboat Institution (RNLI). There has been a lifeboat in St Ives since 1840, and its volunteers have a remarkable record of bravery. In all, 55 awards have been made for gallantry, and seven of its members have lost their lives saving others at sea. The day consists of various stalls to raise money, and the crew take out the lifeboat – currently the *HRH The Princess Royal* (CS No 41) – showing off their launching tractor as well as the speed which can be attained by the lifeboats. All being well the helicopter from RNAS Culdrose (near Helston) may also participate in the festivities, but this depends upon whether or not they need to attend an emergency elsewhere.

The Royal Naval helicopter, and inshore 'D' class lifeboat

Raft Race

The Raft Race is held towards the end of August. It takes place in the evening, and is very well attended by people watching the antics from the harbour side. Teams of people build rafts from various materials, and have to paddle them from the Sloop to each harbour wall, picking up a young lady from one wall and transferring her back to the Sloop; they must also pick up some sort of token to prove they have done the complete circuit. This tends to be an evening of high jinks, with flour bombs and much hilarity. The most highly elaborate rafts tend to lose, but this is certainly one race in which taking part is more important than winning.

St Ives September Festival

The St Ives September Festival celebrates the town's artistic heritage, and is organized over a two-week period in mid-September at various venues in the town. It has existed since 1978, and encompasses a wide range of events including theatre, music and art.

New Year's Eve Celebrations

The New Year's Eve celebrations are not an official event in the town, yet they have grown to such proportions that there is no holding them back! A huge number of people descend upon the town on this evening; the idea is to dress up in fancy-dress and have a good time. What is refreshing about this evening is that it is truly a very good-spirited occasion, with everybody being friendly and happy to show off their costume. But don't be worried about going without fancy-dress, there are plenty of people simply milling around watching the festivities.

The wearing of fancy-dress does have historical connections, though it is difficult to make a direct link between St Ives New Year's Eve celebrations and the Celts who first started the tradition of 'guise dancing'. This, essentially, was the process of dressing up in disguise and having a good time.

It seems fitting to end this book with the New Year's Eve celebrations, where we can all get together and celebrate the town and the start of a new year in characteristic St Ives style: with humour, passion and delight.